Discovering the World Around Us

# Cougars

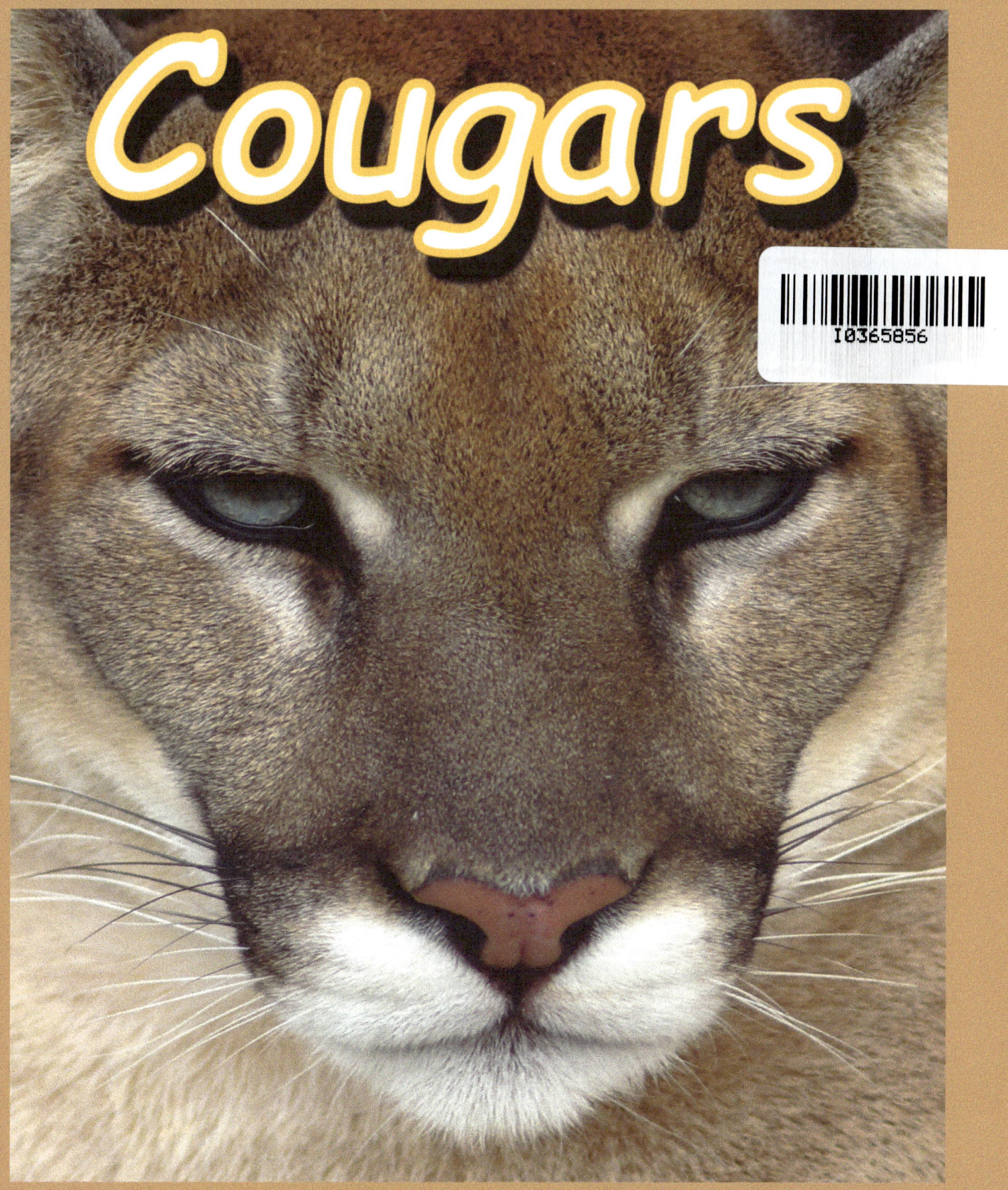

TJ Rob

# COUGARS
By TJ Rob

From the Discovering The World Around Us Series, Volume 5

Copyright Text TJ Rob, 2016
All rights reserved. No part of the book may be reproduced in any form without permission in writing from the author. Reviewers may quote brief passages in review.
ISBN 978-1-988695-15-0

Disclaimer

No part of this book may be reproduced in any form or by any means, mechanical or electronic, including photocopying or recording, or by an information storage and retrieval system, or transmitted by email without permission in writing from the publisher. This book is for entertainment purposes only. The views expressed are those of author alone.

Published by
TJ Rob
Suite 609
440-10816 Macleod Trail SE
Calgary, AB  T2J 5N8  www.TJRob.com

Image Credit:

"Cougar range map 2010" by Kokosdieb - Own work. Licensed under CC BY-SA 3.0 via Commons pg.10

Photo Credits: Images used under license from Shutterstock.com:

Front Cover, L Galbraith/Shutterstock.com; Back Cover, jeep2499/Shutterstock.com; pg. 1, ehtesham/Shutterstock.com; pg. 4, Volodymyr Burdiak/Shutterstock.com; pg. 5, Tom Tietz/Shutterstock.com; pg. 6, Scott E Read/Shutterstock.com; pg. 7, S.R. Maglione/Shutterstock.com; pg. 8, Anan Kaewkhammul/Shutterstock.com; pg. 9, Anan Kaewkhammul/Shutterstock.com; pg. 12, Christopher Gardiner/Shutterstock.com; pg. 15, creativex/Shutterstock.com; pg. 16, outdoorsman/Shutterstock.com; pg. 17, Debbie Steinhausser/Shutterstock.com; pg. 18, Steve Bower/Shutterstock.com; pg. 18, Guoqiang Xue/Shutterstock.com; pg. 18, Tom Reichner/Shutterstock.com; pg. 18, worldswildlifewonders/Shutterstock.com; pg. 18, jadimages/Shutterstock.com; pg. 19, Jody Ann/Shutterstock.com; pg. 19, Tom Reichner/Shutterstock.com; pg. 19, A_Lein/Shutterstock.com; pg. 21, creativex/Shutterstock.com; pg. 22, S.R. Maglione/Shutterstock.com; pg. 23, Jeannette Katzir Photog/Shutterstock.com; pg. 24, Rosalie Kreulen/Shutterstock.com; pg. 25, Louis W Martin/Shutterstock.com; pg. 27, aZiKab/Shutterstock.com; pg. 28, MaZiKab/Shutterstock.com; pg. 29, Scott E Read/Shutterstock.com; pg. 30, Geoffrey Kuchera/Shutterstock.com; pg. 31, welcomia/Shutterstock.com; pg. 32, creativex/Shutterstock.com; pg. 34, Dennis W. Donohue/Shutterstock.com; pg. 37, mlorenz/Shutterstock.com; pg. 39, MaZiKab/Shutterstock.com

| TABLE OF CONTENTS | Page |
|---|---|
| What are Cougars? | 4 |
| Do Cougars have other names that we know them by? | 5 |
| What do Cougars look like? | 6 |
| How big is a Cougar? | 7 |
| How to spot a Cougar... | 8 |
| Where do Cougars live in the wild today? | 11 |
| Where do Cougars like to live? | 13 |
| How many are left in the wild? | 14 |
| How long do Cougars live? | 16 |
| What does a Cougar eat? | 17 |
| Some of the prey that Cougars eat | 18 |
| How often does a Cougar hunt? | 20 |
| How fast can Cougars run? | 22 |
| How far can Cougars jump? | 23 |
| How far do Cougars roam? | 24 |
| What about Cougar babies? | 26 |
| More about Cougar Kittens | 28 |
| Are Cougars dangerous? | 31 |
| How have Cougars adapted to the world they live in? | 33 |
| Cougar fun facts | 36 |
| More Cougar fun facts | 38 |
| Please Leave a REVIEW | 40 |
| Other EXCITING books by TJ Rob | 40 |

## What are Cougars?

Cougars are the largest wild cats in North America and the second largest in South America, after the Jaguar.

They are very secretive and are rarely seen by humans.

Cougars are powerful, agile and are awesome jumpers and climbers.

# Do Cougars have other names that we know them by?

Cougars hold the Guinness record for the animal with the most names — almost 40 different names in English alone.

Cougars are also known as Mountain Lions, Panthers, Pumas and Catamounts.

Because Cougars are found in so many places, the local people and explorers created their own names for this wild cat.

Remember Cougars are not Bobcats, Lynxes, Jaguars, Cheetahs or Leopards.

# What do Cougars look like?

Cougars have similar bodies to house cats, but only much larger.

Cougars have slender bodies and round heads with pointed ears.

The coat of the Cougar is a grayish tan to reddish color with lighter parts on the underside.

The long tail has a black spot on the end.

# How big is a Cougar?

A healthy male Cougar can weigh up to 180 pounds (81 kg), and measure 7 to 8 feet (2.15 to 2.45 meters) long.

An adult male can measure 30 inches (0.2 meter) tall at the shoulder.

Female Cougars are about 3/4 the size of males.

# How to spot a Cougar ...

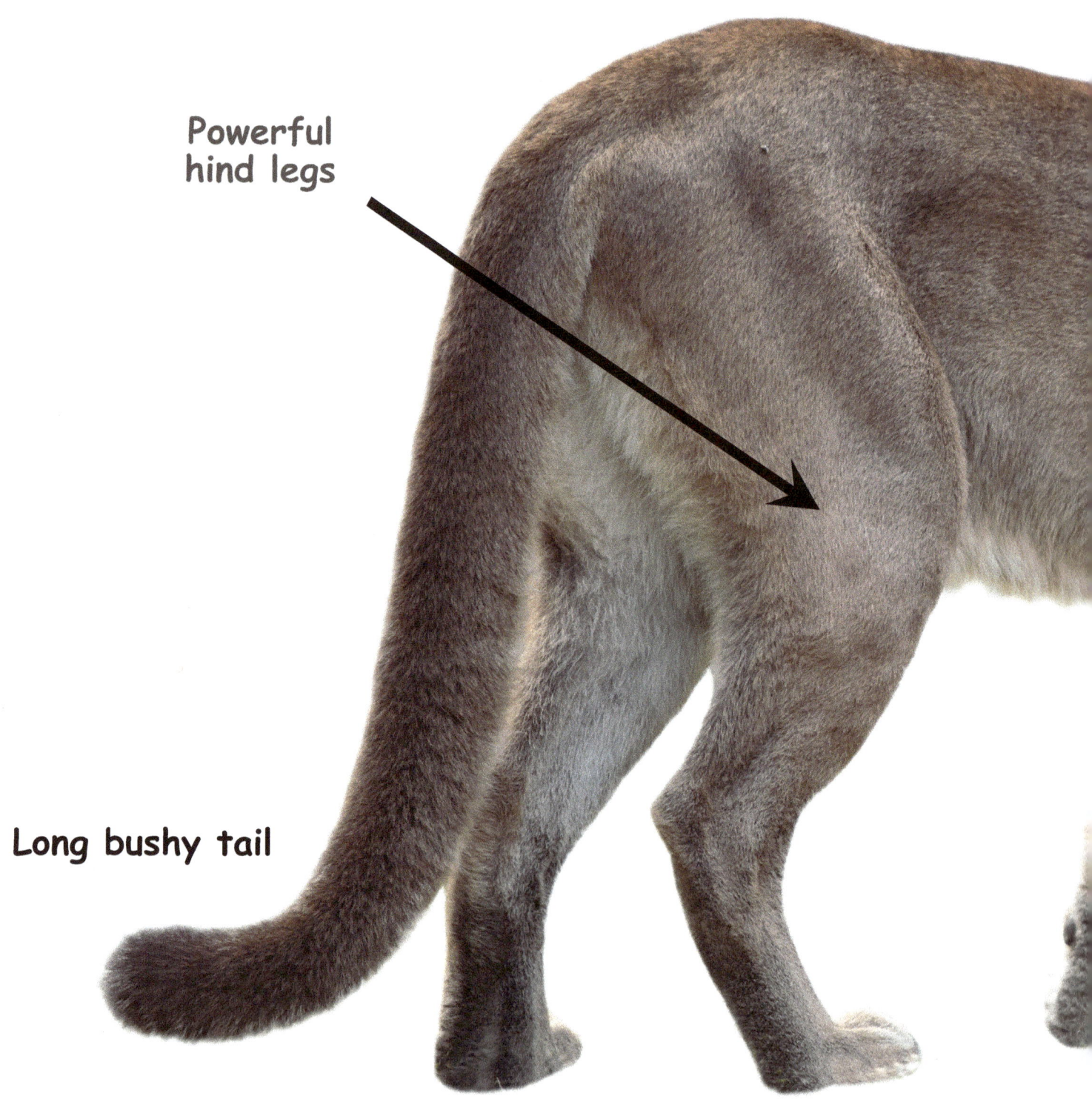

Powerful hind legs

Long bushy tail

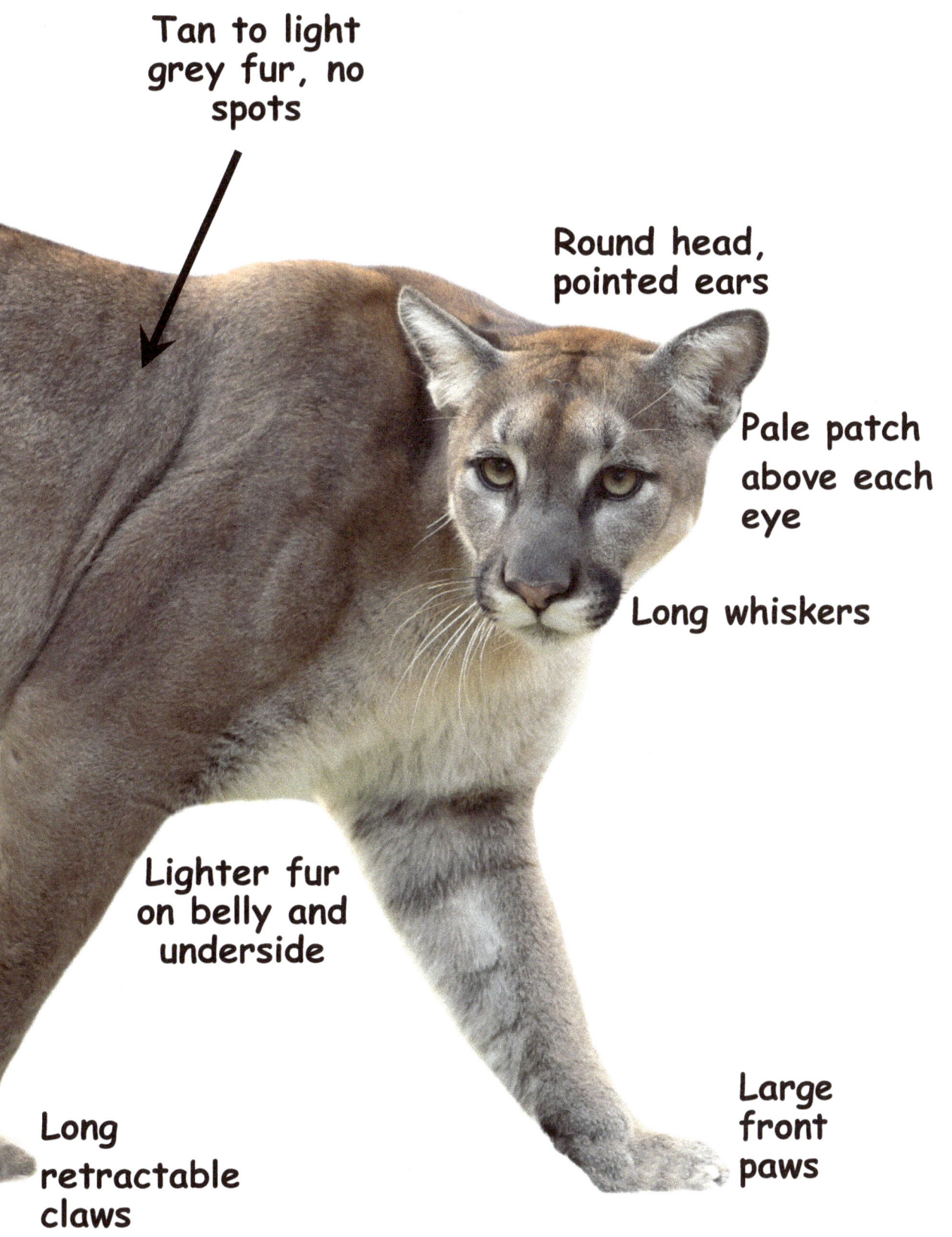

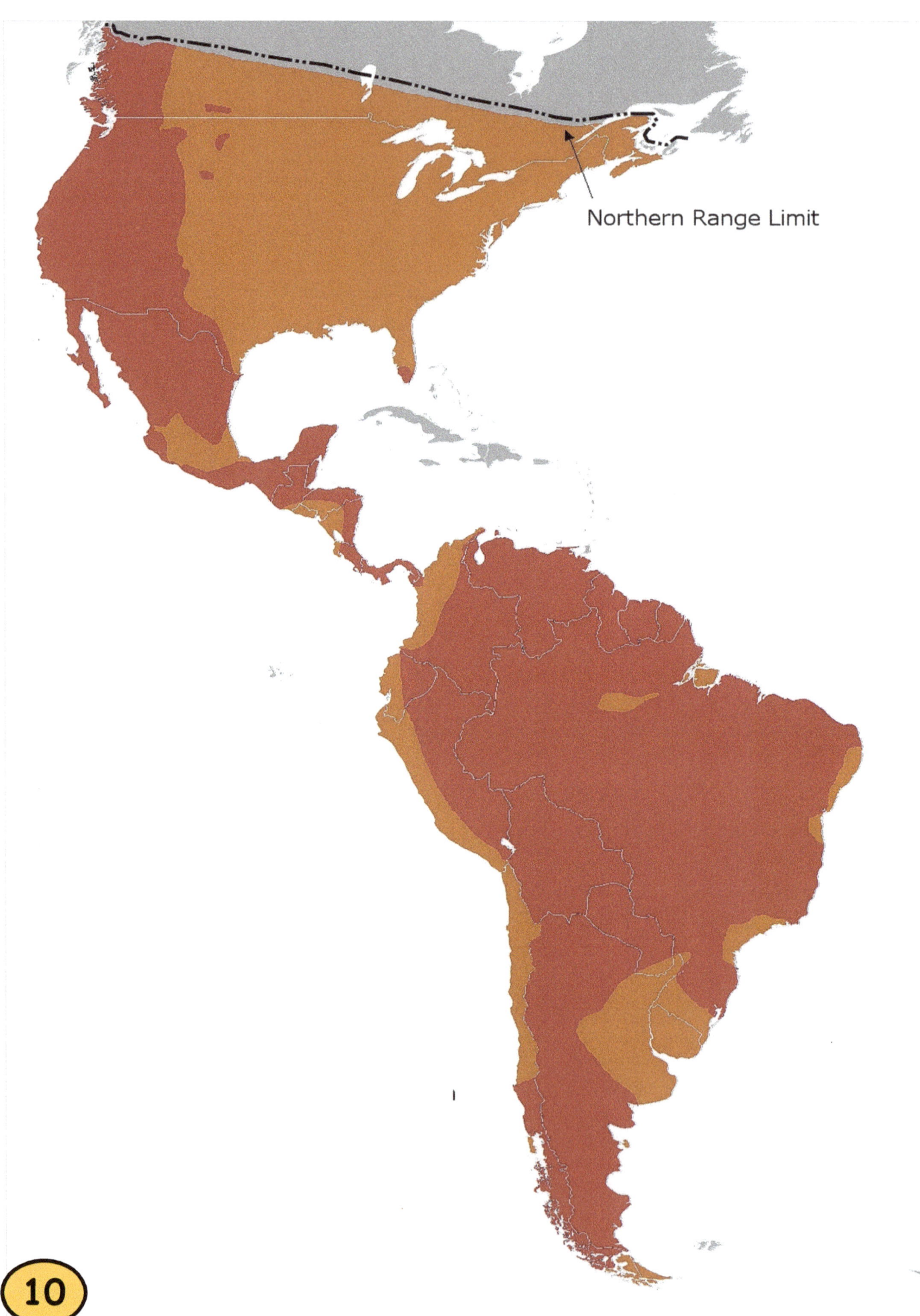

# Where do Cougars live in the wild today?

■ Areas where Cougars live today:

Parts of Western North America, the tip of Florida and most of South America.

■ Areas where Cougars are now extinct or almost extinct.

# Where do Cougars like to live?

Cougars are adaptable to many environments and can be found in low-lying swamps or on high mountain slopes.

They can live near seas or in desert areas.

Cougars don't use dens like bears do. Normally they are on the move, making daybeds as they go.

In rough terrain, daybeds are usually in a cave or a shallow nook on a cliff face or rock outcrop.

In less mountainous areas, daybeds are found in forested areas, dense bush, under large roots or fallen trees.

# How many are left in the wild?

Because Cougars are such shy animals, it is difficult to have an accurate number of how many Cougars are left in the wild.

It is thought that there are about 35,000 to 50,000 animals in the wild.

| | |
|---|---|
| Canada | 3,500 — 5,000 |
| USA | 15,000 — 20,000 |
| South America | 15,000 — 25,000 |

Although Cougars are extinct in most of the Eastern USA, they are starting to return in small numbers.

Cougars are on the Threatened Species list, but they are not in danger of becoming extinct. They fall into the "Least Concern" category on the list — the lowest risk category.

# How long do Cougars live?

In captivity, in zoos and animal sanctuaries, some Cougars are known to live for as long as 20 to 25 years.

The oldest living Cougar in captivity was 30 years old.

# What does a Cougar eat?

Cougars are the least fussy eaters in the cat family.

If it can catch it, Cougars will eat it. Cougars are able to adapt their diet to whatever is available in that area.

They mostly eat deer and mountain sheep.

Cougars are ambush predators. This means that they stalk their prey through the bush and stay hidden until the last moment.

Then using their powerful hind legs, they spring on top of their prey and deliver a killing bite.

# Some of the prey that Cougars eat:

Mule Deer

Bighorn Sheep

Raccoons

Skunks

Armadillos

Beavers

Coyotes

Porcupines

# How often does a Cougar hunt?

Cougars hunt every 10 to 14 days.

This may be as short as once every 3 days for female Cougars that have young to feed.

They hunt from sunset to sunrise — during the night hours — when they can use their amazing eyesight.

After making a kill Cougars drag their prey to a place where they can cover it with brush to hide it.

They will return to this hiding place over the next few days to slowly eat their prey.

# How fast can Cougars run?

Cougars have the largest hind legs in proportion to their bodies of all the big cats.

A Cougar can run at speeds between 40 to 50 miles per hour (60 to 80 km per hour) but is best suited for short sprints rather than long chases.

Over long distances Cougars normally run at about 10 miles per hour (16 km per hour).

# How far can Cougars jump?

With their powerful hind legs, Cougars are great climbers and jumpers.

Cougars ambush their prey animals by leaping down from a distance of 20 to 40 feet (6 to 12 meters).

Cougars have been reported jumping straight up to reach heights of 18 feet (5.5 meters).

# How far do Cougars roam?

Cougars regularly cover hundreds of square miles looking for food.

Unlike other species of cats, Cougars do not live in packs. Instead they live by themselves in large territories.

The only time adult Cougars are together in one place is to mate.

A single Cougar will roam around a territory of about 50 to 150 square miles (80 to 240 square km).

The size of the territory depends on the age of the Cougar and the availability of food.

The less available the food, the bigger the area a Cougar needs to roam to catch it.

# What about Cougar babies?

A baby Cougar is called a kitten or a cub.

A female Cougar has between 1 and 6 kittens in a litter. The average size of a litter is 2 kittens.

A female Cougar is pregnant for about 92 days before having her kittens.

Kittens are born and raised in dens. A den can be in a cave, a crack between rocks, hollows under tree roots, or a hidden spot in dense bush. The den is sometimes lined with moss or other plants, and might be used for a few years.

Cougar kittens are completely helpless at birth. They are born with their ears and eyes closed,

After about 2 weeks they are able to hear and see.

# More about Cougar kittens

Kittens are born with blackish-brown spotted coats. The spotted coats help to hide the kittens from predators.

These spots begin to fade at about 12 to 14 weeks.

They continue to fade as the kitten gets older.

The spots are completely gone in about 18 months.

Cougar mothers are very protective of their kittens.

Cougar mothers have been known to fight off Grizzly bears to protect their young.

By 2 to 3 months old, the kittens no longer need their mother's milk and are ready to eat solid food.

When raising kittens, the mother Cougar will leave them alone for short periods of time as she hunts for food.

In the beginning she will hunt close to the den, but as the kittens grow she will go out further.

Kittens remain with their mother until they are independent at about 15 to 24 months of age.

Once independent, they scatter over large distances to seek out their own territories.

Female Cougars are ready to have their own kittens between 18 months and 3 years of age.

# Are Cougars dangerous?

Even though Cougars do live in many areas inhabited by humans, they avoid humans whenever possible.

Attacks on humans by Cougars are very rare.

Fatal Cougar attacks on humans are less frequent than fatal dog attacks, fatal snake bites, fatal lightning strikes or even fatal bee stings.

There have been less than 30 deaths in North America by Cougars over the last 125 years.

Like all predators, Cougars attack when they are cornered or to protect their kittens.

They also will attack if they believe you are about to steal their catch that they have hidden away.

# How have Cougars adapted to the world they live in?

Super sensitive hearing. Cougars can hear sounds that humans are not able to.

They can also turn each ear separately to locate where a sound is coming from. This helps to find their prey.

Amazing eyesight that is 6 times better than humans in poor light. This gives Cougars a big advantage when hunting at night.

Powerful jaws that can crush the neck or strangle their prey in a single bite.

# How have Cougars adapted to the world they live in?

Large paws with soft padding help the Cougar walk softly to stalk its prey, and to swat the rear legs of its prey in a chase.

A long tail helps the Cougar balance on high rocky ledges and up in the trees.

A Cougar uses its long tail like a rudder when it wants to change direction during a chase.

Powerful hind legs that help the Cougar jump and climb.

# Cougar Fun Facts

1. Cougars cannot roar like Lions. Cougars make a lot of different sounds. They make whistling sounds, they squeak, purr, hiss, growl, and even make a chuckling sound.

    Female Cougars make a screaming sound during mating season that sounds like a woman's scream.

    Cougars are the largest cat that can purr.

2. A Cougar's tail is really long. A Cougar's tail can be the same length as the rest of the body and the head combined.

3. Cougars are pretty good swimmers. They will follow Deer into water and will mostly outswim them and catch them.

    Canadian Cougars have been known to swim from one coastal island to another.

# More Cougar Fun Facts

4. Cougar kittens have blue eyes. It takes about 16 months for their eyes to become the greenish yellow color that adult Cougars have.

5. The size of a Cougar depends on where on the continent it is found. Cougars found closer to the Equator are smaller. Cougars found closer to the North and South Poles are larger. The size increases the closer to the Poles that a Cougar is found.

6. Cougars are the most successful hunters of all the big cats. Lions only catch 10% of the prey that they hunt. Cougars are far more successful. Cougars will catch 80% of the prey that they hunt.

# THANKS FOR READING!

Please leave a review at the website where you bought this book and tell others what you liked about it.

Visit www.TJRob.com for a FREE eBook and to see TJ Rob's other exciting books

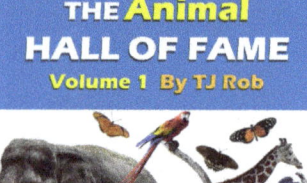

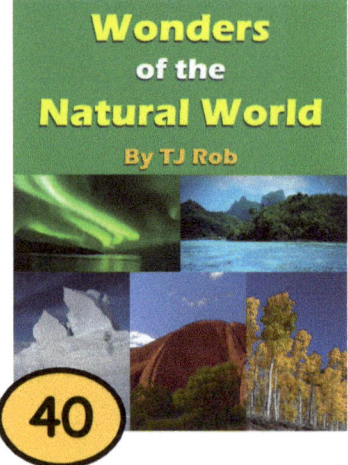
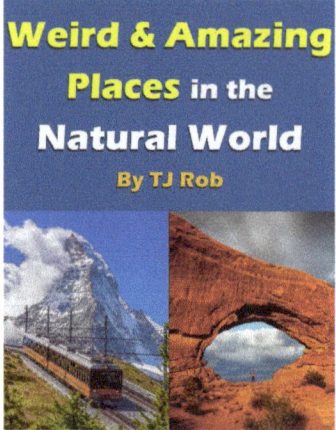

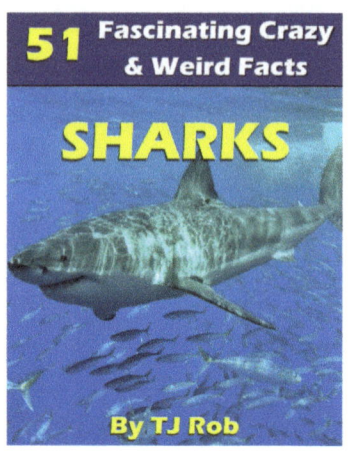

www.ingramcontent.com/pod-product-compliance
Lightning Source LLC
Chambersburg PA
CBHW040004080526
44586CB00027B/2883